The Trials and
Tribulations
of Landlords
against professional
Tenants

Comfort Addy

About the Author

Comfort is a first-time writer, a generous and kind-hearted property owner, and a passionate advocate for small landlords. With firsthand experience navigating the challenges of landlord-tenant relationships, she has faced the struggles of dealing with problematic tenants head-on. Her journey has inspired her to share valuable insights and lessons learned, helping others avoid similar pitfalls in property management.

Driven by her current experiences with professional tenants, Comfort is becoming a dedicated activist for small landlord homeowners—many of whom face financial ruin due to professional tenants who exploit the system. Through her writing, she aims to raise awareness, advocate for fair housing policies, and empower fellow landlords with practical advice and support.

When she's not writing, she enjoys researching solutions for fair housing practices and finding new ways to help landlords protect their investments and peace of mind.

Dedication

This book is dedicated to every landlord who has suffered at the hands of professional tenants, those who exploited the system, drained your finances, and stole your peace of mind.

It is for those who built a future, only to see it unravel due to deceitful tenants and flawed legal systems. May you find solace in knowing you are not alone, strength in the lessons learned, and hope for a better path forward. Your resilience tells a story worth sharing.

United, we stand fighting this cause created by our government, so please do not relent. Talk, share, and expose the system for what it is.

ACKNOWLEDGMENT:

A heartfelt thank you to my publisher, McGilligan Publishing Group, for their unwavering guidance and support in bringing this book to life. Your expertise, patience, and dedication have been invaluable throughout this journey. From refining my ideas to shaping them into a compelling narrative, your insight and encouragement have made all the difference.

Thank you for believing in this project and for helping me navigate the complexities of publishing with professionalism and care. This book would not have been possible without your commitment to sharing important stories with the world. I am deeply grateful for your role in making this vision a reality. Big shout out to Daniel White, Emma Parker, Sarah Parker, Priscilla Tessa and others not mentioned.

Table of Content

Preface

This is a brief account of the challenges I have faced as a small landlord and homeowner, the missteps I encountered, and key lessons on what to do and what to avoid when striving to become a successful and profitable landlord.

Chapter 1: The Challenges Landlords Face Before Owning a Rental Property

The story begins with a landlord striving to make ends meet, seeking a loan, and searching for the ideal property to generate rental income. After navigating the rigorous loan approval process, the next challenge is identifying a property that aligns with their investment goals. Once purchased, the uphill battle continues, coordinating with contractors to renovate and prepare the unit, all while hoping to secure reliable tenants. In my case, after overcoming these hurdles, I transformed an unfinished basement into a beautifully completed living space.

Here's the Basement Unfinished: 👇

After completing these extensive improvements, the next challenge was securing the right tenants. The upper unit attracted responsible renters who moved in without issue. Then came a young woman, let's call her Yumpy, who claimed to be a single mother relying on social benefits. With charm, persuasive assurances, and a desperate plea for shelter for herself and her baby, she presented herself as stable and reliable. Convinced by her story, I granted her the lease, believing I had found an ideal tenant.

Chapter 2: The Unwelcome Additions

Within days, the situation took a turn. Yumpy had misrepresented her circumstances; she was not alone. Her partner, who worked full-time, moved in with her despite not being listed on the lease. What was supposed to be a peaceful rental quickly became a source of chaos, with constant noise, heated arguments, and late-night disturbances disrupting the entire property.

Yumpy turned the unit from Beauty to Chaos, and that was the beginning of the Landlord's Nightmare: The once beautifully finished basement, carefully renovated before the tenant surfaced, quickly transformed from a dream to a disaster. In addition to completing the basement, I invested heavily in upgrading the upper unit, replacing the roof, fixing windows, repainting the entire house, and repairing the deck and balcony. The list of renovations seemed endless for a landlord like me. Other tenants moved into the unit above Yumpy and so was the escalation of the chaos on the property.

Chapter 3: Driving Away the Good Tenants

As the disturbances escalated, the tenant's behavior became more destructive. Late-night yelling, crying, and bickering became routine, with no regard for the other occupants. Property damage soon followed, and the once beautifully finished basement, renovated with care, was reduced to a filthy, unrecognizable state, resembling a garbage dump.

What started as a promising investment turned into a landlord's worst nightmare. BEFORE👇

So the beautifully finished basement given to this tenant suddenly went from beauty to beast.

Now👇

The living room became a toilet haven for her dog; the floors are littered with dog pee.

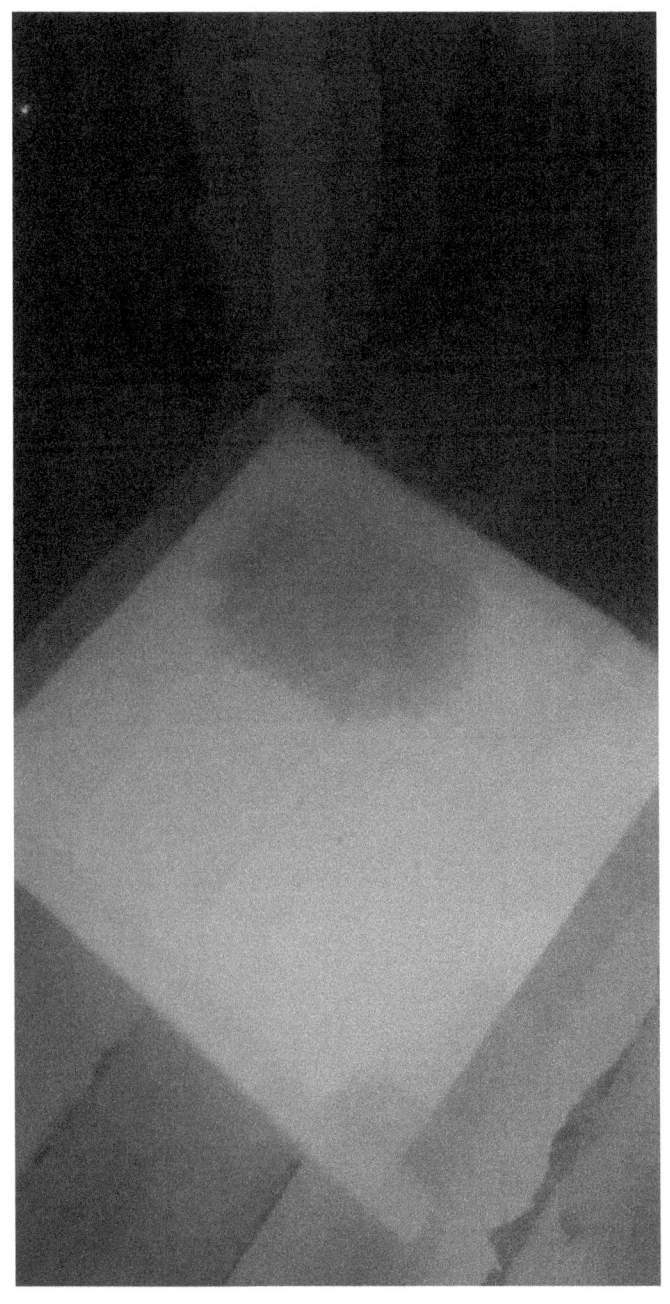

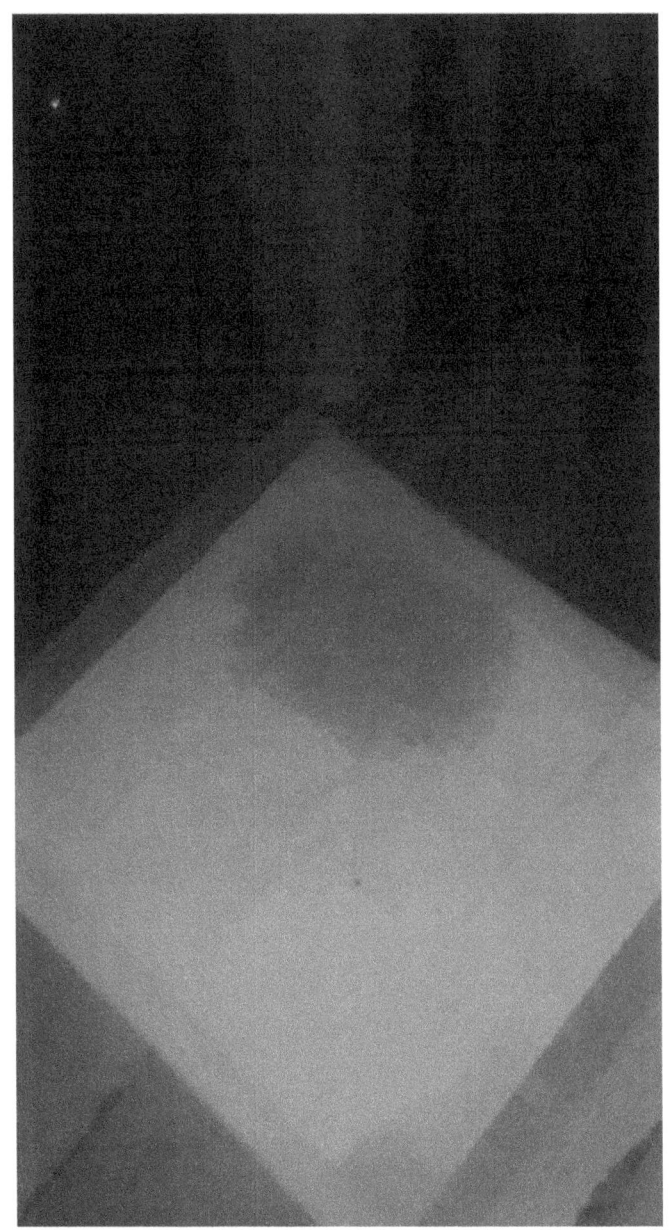

Beautifully renovated bedroom went from bright

to darkness👀👇

The hallway that was glossy, shiny, and beautiful was turned into a hidden area for God knows what (looks like drug hidden arena).

Before:

Now👇

Beautifully renovated washroom, which the landlord put her soul to decorate to her delight, became like a Halloween decorated hall, a place looking like the ones you see in a horror movie:

Before 👇

Now 👇

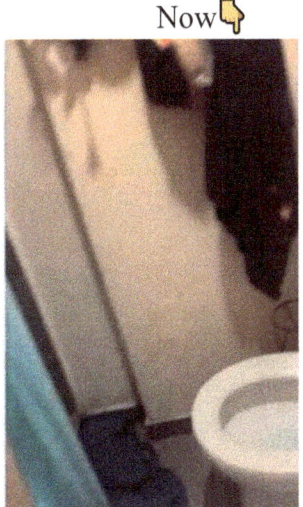

Before👇

Now: 👇

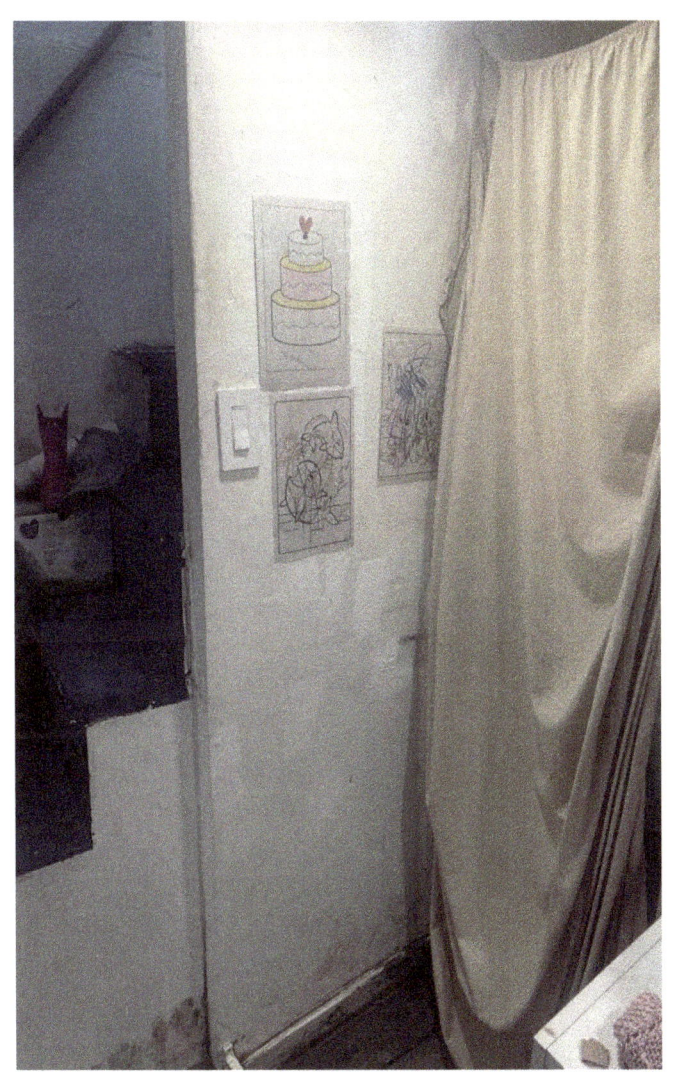

Toilet with beautiful door

were ripped out. Why she did this is beyond explanation

The walls were massacred as if they used machetes:

Window blinds were mangled and became a hangar; how that became a hanging spot is still a shock unbelievable to get over.

Some parts of the walls were cut into maybe to hide drugs:

BEFORE👇

Now 👇

The big question is, why was the wall added to? What is behind that wall is a million-dollar question that can be asked when the tenant is eventually evicted. The appliances were damaged beyond control, fridge was ripped out of the whole unit:

BEFORE 👇

Now 👇

doors are ripped off the hinge:👇

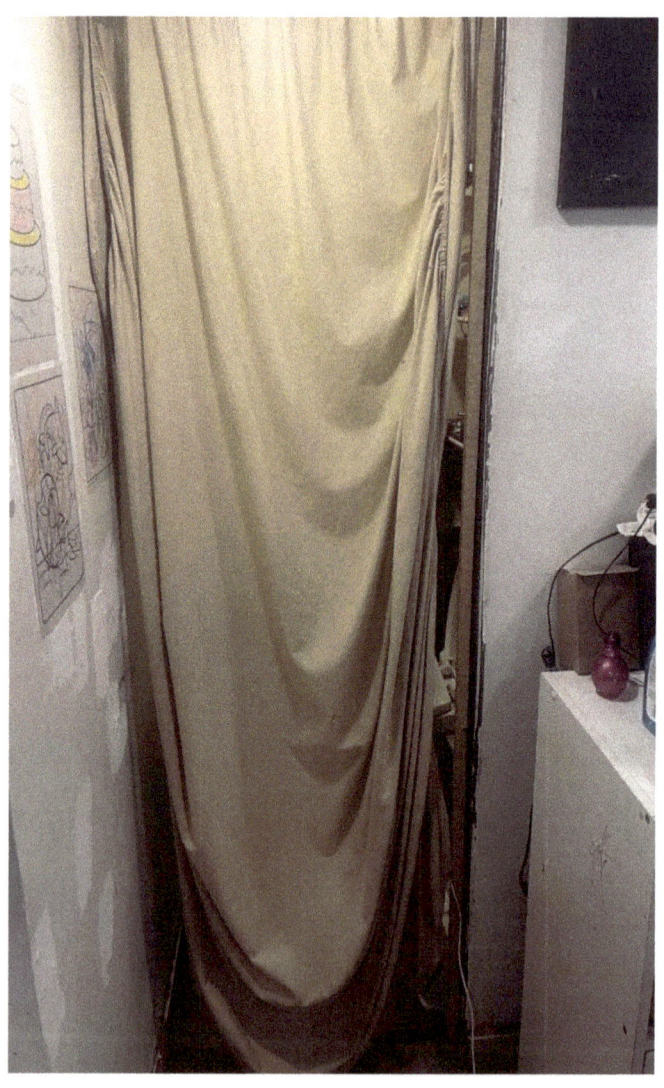

and window blinds were mangled as if tornadoes just touched down in the apartment

Their actions and reactions sent loyal, amazing, well-behaved tenants away. Most were frustrated by the worsening environment and began moving out. The landlord's rental business was left in shambles, with a vacant unit and a tarnished reputation on the street.

Chapter 4: The Drug Problem Uncovered.

It wasn't long before the landlord discovered the tenant and her partner were struggling with substance abuse. This revelation added a dangerous element to the situation. Drug-related activity at the property raised concerns about safety and legal liability. The landlord's stress levels soared as they struggled to regain control. Not only was it realized that they were on drugs, but they were even on prescribed drugs to wean them off the hard substances they were taking. These couples unfortunately have a little girl growing up in the middle of these mayhems. The action of the government agency allowing this little girl to grow up in this kind of environment is more than unimaginable.

When the landlord realized all this mayhem, he decided to give notice to the tenant and her unapproved co-habitant, and that was the beginning of the problem between the landlord, the said tenant, her spouse, her mother-in-law, and even they involved the little girl. They started throwing tantrums, started with bullying tactics, calling police and firefighters ceaselessly on the property in order to dissuade the landlord from evicting them: Fire department constant

visit

Despite all their threats and intimidations, the landlord took their case to the only entity that could resolve the issue and evict these professional renters, and that is the entity called: "Landlord and Tenant Board." So landlord and tenant's board were called, and the landlord was told to issue several N forms to warn them, but none of the warnings worked as the tenants continued with terrorist acts on the property, and constant bullying by them became the daily norm. Name-calling became their anthem by constantly using racist names and calling the landlord a foreigner, so eventually, the landlord was asked to give them another N form, which, this time, was the landlord's wish to move her family in, but this professional tenant still refused to move out so the landlord who kept raking debts upon debts monthly on the said property decided to put the house for sale so the house was put on MLS costing the owner another thousand of dollars to be advertised online.

The house was snatched up in less time, with the buyer stipulating that she wanted the whole house to herself, so the landlord and tenants board was called again, explaining the situation at hand to them, and was told to give the tenant another N12 specifying house sale with purchaser's intention to keep the whole house for their family and was done with the intention that the tenant and her supposed spouse will respect the landlord's wish this time but lo and behold, the tenant said her lawyer told her that the new owner must assume her.

Chapter 5: All Attempts to Evict Fail:

As with all attempts by the landlord to evict this professional tenant and her unauthorized occupant, I was left with no choice but to take the tenant to the Landlord-Tenant Board, file the L2 application to evict this tenant, and after that, the wait started. The said tenants knew all the rules, formulations, and regulations of the board. She proudly boasted to the landlord that there was nothing she could do as the board would take more than 6 months before responding and that after those times, she'd still find ways to delay sending her out of the unit, that was when the reality of dealing with the Landlord and Tenant Board (LTB) hit hard.

The landlord discovered the process was slow, complex, and heavily weighted in favor of tenants, even those who blatantly violated agreements. This particular tenant has been in the unit she destroyed from top to bottom for nearly four years but refuses to leave because, according to her spouse, they couldn't find any other apartment because (1) they're expensive, (2) No one wants to rent to them which makes me wonder which landlord in his or her right minds will ever house these type of people.

Chapter 6: Lessons Learned:

The experience left the landlord with valuable, albeit painful, lessons: Monies were lost, peace of mind eroded the landlord, and the pain of looking at how once the beautiful unit was turned into a dumpster garage is too heartbroken to be fathomed therefore, after having gone through these horrible experiences, I discovered that there are 20 essential rules that must be followed when renting out to tenants and here they are:

20 GUIDELINES TO FOLLOW WHEN RENTING YOUR UNIT/UNITS

(1) Never rent to any tenant under any circumstances until you do a **thorough Screening.** This is highly Essential: (a)Never take a tenant's word at face value. Verify income and references, especially check and recheck criminal background. Had it been that I checked the criminal background of this particular tenant, I wouldn't be in this mess while going through this ordeal now decided to check her background, I found that she's a hardened criminal who had been convicted of fraud where she was caught for cashing innocent people's cheques more than one time:

Niagara Falls Review
https://www.niagarafallsreview.ca › ...

In the courts

Sep 2, 2016 — ▓▓▓▓▓▓▓▓▓▓▓▓▓▓ pleaded guilty Friday in an Ontario Court of Justice in St. Catharines to charges of fraud under $5,000 and ...

(2) **Check rigorously** and do a drug test if you suspect they have drug problems before ever giving your key to any tenants, especially those on social benefits. After checking recently about this particular tenant, the former tenants were able to snitch about her and how they are on Methadone, which is a strong solution given by a medical doctor to wean them off opioid addiction.

(3) **Clear Lease Agreements:** Make sure to include detailed clauses about who is allowed to reside on the property and enforce them. As soon as you find out they're doing or going contrary to what is stipulated, warn them right away, and if that fails, start legal action against them right away. Leaving situations unresolved like mine for so long makes the tenants grow wing and so difficult to control or send out of your property.

(4) **Be Proactive**: Address red flags immediately, whether it's noise complaints or unauthorized occupants. Several complaints were made about this tenant and her unlawful spouse, but I took their word for it because each time I confronted them, they always denied it. The realization dawned on me after the last tenant was driven out, and I decided to stay in the house; I realized that they're actually much more horrible than I was told. They, including the 3+ years old little girl, always start their shenanigans of yelling, crying, and fighting every single night. It was so horrible and nauseating that police had to be called several times.

(5) **Know the Law:** Understand landlord-tenant regulations to protect yourself and your property. Decide on whether to sign a one-year lease, month to month or share accommodation; knowing the rules will make you know what to do and how to go about it. Be well aware

that these professional tenants know the in and out of these rules and use them to their advantage, so protect your assets by making sure you know all that is need to know.

(6) **Verify and re-verify references** to clear up fake ones.

(7) **Do financial background checks** to know their credit scores, if they don't have good credit scores, let them explain why and hold them to their reasons.

(8) **Specify who the occupants are,** and if they bring any additional tenants they must ask for permission and that there'll be additional charges.

(9) **Make them pay for the utility bills;** when utility bills are paid by the tenants, they tend to conserve electricity and or gas usage.

(10) **Stay away from smokers,** and if you must take smokers as tenants, make it bold and clear of no smoking policy in the house if there is, reiterate that there'll be an extra charge for cleaning and

(11) **Do regular inspections** of the house at least twice a year, this will let you detect what is going on in the house as soon as it starts

(12) **Seek Professional Help**: Enlist for the help of a lawyer who knows well about real estate or if you can't afford it, look for help with paralegals who will charge less than a real estate lawyer. Doing these will lighten your problems and can help you navigate difficult situations and mediate conflicts.

(13) **Police reports:** Obtain police reports on them by all means to have an idea of who they are

(14) **Tenant Insurance**: The tenants must have tenant insurance, so in case of damage, you'll bear no responsibility for their belongings.

(15) **Transfer the utilities to their names**, It is highly essential to transfer it to their names so they can they can be responsible for their own bill payments.

(16) **Make them sign up to get a smoke detector alarm** and promise to change the battery themselves every 3 months.

(17) **Make them sign no breach of contract** so you can have a way to make them responsible through the breach of contract if they do so.

(18) **Do Credit checks on them**

(19) **Make them sign a Promissory note** to leave after 1 year

(20) **Make them sign that you're going to be checking the property** at least twice a year.

If you can't do all these, seek the help of a property manager who has more knowledge and has more hands on knowing how to deal with tenants especially the difficult ones like we have in this episode.

Chapter 7: A Warning to Fellow Landlords:

The story is still ongoing, and I am praying and hoping that it ends well so I can write a subsequent book after this. My heartfelt pleas to other landlords are to:

I.   Protect yourselves and your investments. Never be too friendly to any tenants: remember this is your business, not family or friendly affairs.

II. Make all your household rules legible and state facts to be followed so there'll be no confusion as to what is what; remember to remind yourself that even though the system may seem to favor tenants, by being vigilant, thorough, and informed, you can avoid similar trials and tribulations.

III. The rental business isn't as simple as it seems. Even good intentions can backfire, so stay informed, and never underestimate the challenges of being a landlord.

Epilogue

Though my journey as a landlord has been filled with trials and tribulations, I've gained invaluable lessons. Sharing my story is my way of turning adversity into something meaningful. If my experience helps even one landlord avoid similar struggles, it will be worth it. Even as painful as it is to lose so much with this particular tenant, I still believe it'll be a good idea to give some positive advice to tenants or would-be tenants on how to navigate the renting phase of their lives; that is why I'm giving these advices below:

Here are 10 uplifting pieces of advice for tenants to help them improve their situation and relationships with landlords:

1. **Respect Your Home and Treat your rental as if you owned it.** A well-maintained home makes life more comfortable and keeps your landlord and yourself happy.

2. **Pay Rent on Time.** It's a simple yet powerful habit. Paying on time builds trust and keeps you stress-free; remember, your landlord has to pay banks or mortgage lenders as well.

3. **Communicate Honestly** when you're facing difficulties, talk to your landlord early. Honesty can lead to solutions instead of conflicts.

4. **Follow and respect the Lease Agreement.** It's there for a reason. Respecting the rules avoids unnecessary drama and potential legal trouble.

5. **Be a Good Neighbor.** A peaceful living environment benefits everyone. Keep noise levels reasonable and be considerate to others.

6.   **Take Care of Repairs Quickly** by reporting small issues before they become big and costly problems. It saves you and the landlord from headaches.

7.   **Keep It Clean.** A clean home is a happy home. Regular upkeep prevents pests, mold, and other issues that could cost you your security deposit and endanger your health.

8.   **Be Responsible with Guests**. Enjoy your space, but be mindful of who you bring in and how they behave. You're responsible for their actions.

9.   **Plan Your Move-Out Properly and give proper notice,** clean up, and return keys as agreed. Leaving on good terms can secure a great reference for your next home.

10. **Change Your Mindset.** If you've had issues as a tenant before, view this as an opportunity for a fresh start. Small improvements in taking care of your responsibilities can make life much easier.

Being a great tenant not only benefits the landlord but benefits you as well because you'll be able to get good references for the next apartment you'll be going to or even get good tips on how to acquire your first home from the Landlord who has quite an array of experiences.

The benefits of having good relationships with your landlord and vice versa are astounding and will make life easier for all parties involved. Remember the saying Happy home, happy life. **THE END**